MALLARD PRESS

An imprint of BDD Promotional Books Company, Inc.,
666 Fifth Avenue, New York, N.Y. 10103

Mallard Press and its accompanying design and logo
are trademarks of BDD Promotional Book Company, Inc.

CLB 2344

First published in the United States of America
in 1990 by The Mallard Press
Printed and bound in Italy by Fratelli Spada, SpA

ISBN 0 792 45033 7

· Oxford Scientific Films ·

REPTILES

Mike Linley

Contents

Previous page: a western ringnecked snake. The feet of the chameleon (left) are perfect for gripping.

1

What is a Reptile?

There are some 6,500 species of reptiles known to science. Of these, over 2,000 are snakes, nearly 4,000 are lizards, around 250 are chelonians (tortoises, turtles and terrapins) and twenty-two are crocodilians. There is also a strange, lizard-like reptile called the tuatara, which is in a separate group all on its own.

Reptiles, like their close relatives the *amphibians*, are cold blooded, that is to say they do not produce enough heat to keep their bodies at a constant temperature as birds and mammals do. This means that a reptile can live on a fraction of the food needed by a similarly-sized mammal and so survive in areas such as deserts, where there is little food available.

The tuatara, and many species of lizard, has a third "eye" on top of the head. Known as the pineal, it helps the reptile to judge the amount of sunshine available so it can bask in the sun to keep warm.

Reptiles are covered in hard, horny scales made of *keratin*. These serve not only to protect the animal against being eaten, especially in reptiles like the tortoise, but also to prevent water being lost through the skin by *evaporation*.

Some lizards, like the green basilisk (top), have crests, spines or frills. Left: a thick-tailed gecko shedding its skin.

In order to grow, reptiles have periodically to shed the outer layer of their skin. This also enables them to replace damaged scales and rid themselves of external parasites such as ticks and mites.

Most reptiles are four-legged, except in the case of snakes and legless lizards, but there are some worm-lizards in Mexico which have only two front legs and some skinks in Australia which only have two back legs!

Lizards, snakes and crocodiles possess teeth, but tortoises, turtles and terrapins are completely toothless. Instead they have a thick, sharp ridge of horny keratin along their upper and lower jaws. When these two ridges meet they act like a pair of shears, slicing off leaves or flesh.

Left: the juvenile, yellow, stage of the green tree python, and (below) a green spiny lizard, found in woodland in Costa Rica.

2
The Tuatara

At first glance the tuatara looks like a large, crested lizard. It is, however, the only surviving member of a group of reptiles that lived over 150 million years ago. They were called the rhynchocephalians (*rhyncho* meaning beak, and *cephalus* meaning head) or beak-heads because of the shape of their skull. Sixty-five million years ago they had all died out, except for the tuatara.

Many people refer to the tuatara as a "living fossil." Today it lives on a number of small islands around New Zealand, and it is probably due to the complete isolation that the tuatara has survived here for so long. Many of the islands are very damp and often shrouded in fog, a strange *habitat* for a usually sun-loving reptile, but the tuatara is nocturnal and active at much lower temperatures than snakes or lizards.

The tuatara feeds on insects, snails, small lizards and possibly the sea bird chicks with which it shares its burrows. It is particularly fond of the weta, a type of giant cricket unique to New Zealand.

Male tuataras are very territorial and always on the look-out for intruders. Should a rival male wander into his territory, the resident male will erect its spiky crest along its neck and back and begin to strut up and down in a threatening manner. Rivals rarely come to blows.

Female tuataras lay their dozen or so eggs in

A male tuatara.

a shallow pit in the soft soil. On Stephens Island they have a habit of nesting in the lighthouse keeper's vegetable garden, where it is easier to dig! The eggs take around fifteen months to hatch, a remarkably long time.

Tuataras live on islands around New Zealand.

A lizard egg normally hatches within two or three months. On hatching, the four-inch-long tuataras are tiny replicas of their parents and feed on small insects, such as young wetas. They grow very slowly and may take thirty years to reach maturity.

Tuataras are known to reach a ripe old age of 120 years or more. Adult tuataras have very few enemies, but the eggs and young can be eaten by rats, which were introduced into New Zealand from Europe. If rats found their way to the tiny islands it would spell disaster for the reptiles. The New Zealand Government, however, takes every precaution to protect this rare and unusual reptile.

3

Lizards

With nearly 4,000 species, the lizards are the largest family of reptiles. Except for the Arctic and Antarctic, lizards are found throughout the world, from Scandinavia in the north to Tierra del Fuego in the south, from sea level to some 5,000 feet in altitude. They vary in size from tiny geckos, barely an inch long, to the gigantic Komodo dragon, which can reach ten feet in length and weighs over three hundred and fifty pounds. They can be found living in almost every type of habitat, from deserts to swamps, as well as under ground, in trees, in rocky crevices and even around houses. Only one species, the marine iguana of the Galápagos Islands, has successfully conquered the sea. It spends its day basking on the rocky shore between dives beneath the waves to feed on seaweed.

Although there are a number of *herbivorous* lizards, the vast majority are either *carnivorous* or *insectivorous*. Some species are highly specialized in their choice of prey. The North American horned "toad" (it is in fact a lizard) feeds almost exclusively on ants, while the thorny devil of Australia specializes in termites and the caiman lizard from Guyana eats snails.

Lizards differ from snakes in many ways, the obvious one being that most lizards possess legs. They usually have ears, visible as either a hole on either side of the head, or as a large scale. Lizards' eyes are normally protected by eyelids, while those of snakes cannot be closed and are instead covered by clear, circular scales.

Many lizards have very special feet. Geckoes generally have flattened toes that are covered along their undersides by rows of thousands of minute hairs. The hairs end in hooks that latch onto the cracks and ridges on leaves, branches and walls. They allow the gecko to run upside down along a ceiling or even up a sheet of glass.

Many desert-living species have fingers of scales along their digits, enabling the animal to run over loose sand. The chameleon has its fingers fused together, two on one side and three on the other, like a mitten, so allowing it to grip firmly onto branches.

Lizards are among the few reptiles that actually make a noise. Geckoes are often called chitchats in many parts of the world because of the chattering noise they make. The huge, twelve-inch tokay gecko gets its name from its raucous call – "to-kay," while the little barking gecko sits at the entrance to its sandy burrow calling to its neighbors.

The Galápagos land iguana (left) feeds mainly on cacti. The specially adapted toes of the tokay gecko (facing page top) enable it to climb up surfaces as smooth as glass. The ameiva lizard (facing page bottom) is usually found in sunny clearings in rainforests.

4
Snakes

Like their close relatives the lizards, snakes are found throughout the world outside the polar regions. (There are, however, two notable exceptions – the islands of Ireland and New Zealand have never been colonized by snakes.) These reptiles vary in size from the tiny thread snakes, which are barely six inches long, to the gigantic pythons, which can reach over thirty-six feet in length. Snakes differ from lizards mainly in the things they lack, such as legs, eyelids and external ears.

The snake's most striking feature is its elongated body, which normally accounts for around four-fifths of its total length. Within the body there are between two and four hundred ribs protecting the vital organs inside. Needless to say, in a body of this shape, the internal organs have to be formed and reorganized in order to fit. The snake's kidneys are long and thin, and one lies in front of the other instead of side by side. In most species there is only one long, thin lung, the other, usually the left one, is either much smaller or else completely absent.

Snakes move in several different ways, but the typical serpentine locomotion is used by most species. This involves the reptile moving in a series of S-bends, pushing against the ground, or other objects, with several parts of its body at the same time, so forcing it forward. The larger, thicker-bodied species tend to adopt the "rib-walking" technique. For this, blocks of the large scales that cover the animal's underside are

Below left: an Indian green tree snake.
Below: a young eyelash viper lies in wait for hummingbirds.

raised, moved forward and pushed against the ground so the snake "concertinas" forward in a more-or-less straight line.

The sidewinding rattlesnake of North America and the sidewinding viper of the Namib Desert have each evolved exactly the same method of locomotion to cope with life in their very similar habitats. Each species spends its life moving over loose sand, where moving by either "serpentine" or "rib-walking" locomotion would be very difficult. Instead they have learnt to throw themselves forward in a series of coils in such a way that much of the body does not even touch the sand (which very often is too hot to touch!). The tracks they leave behind are unmistakably those of a sidewinder. Most snakes travel at between two and four miles per hour, and the fastest is probably the African black mamba, which has been timed moving at over seven miles an hour.

The snakes have one other feature which sets them apart from the rest of the reptiles: the bones of the jaws are held together only by muscles and tendons, so they are able to move a great distance apart from each other. The snake is able to stretch its mouth over prey much thicker than the diameter of its own head. Swallowing such large prey means these reptiles only need to feed occasionally, sometimes only twice a month in many species.

The python (above) has a thick, muscular body. The sidewinder (below) has developed a strange way of moving over sand.

5
Crocodiles and Alligators

There are twenty-two species of crocodilian spread across the warmer regions of the Americas, Africa, Asia and Australia. They vary in size from the relatively tiny African dwarf crocodile, at five feet in length, to the gigantic saltwater crocodile of Australasia. These monstrous creatures can be twenty-five feet long, and are among the few reptiles that have been known to kill and eat humans.

The crocodilians are the last reminder of the great dinosaurs and have remained more or less unchanged for the past sixty-five million years. They are always found in or close to water. Much of the day is spent lazing in the sun, soaking up the warmth. During the evening they become active and start to hunt for food. Small crocodiles and alligators feed on insects, fish, amphibians and snails, but as they grow they tend to eat more and more mammals. Many of these are taken when they come to the water's edge to drink. The crocodile's nostrils, ears and eyes are all placed at the same level along the top of its

The Indian gharial (above) feeds mainly on fish. American alligators (right) once faced extinction, but are now becoming more numerous in Florida.

head. This allows the crocodile to submerge all but a small part of its body and head and still be able to see, hear and breathe. Even the part that is visible above the water resembles a floating log and enables the crocodile to approach the drinking animal without being seen. The prey is then seized in a powerful pair of jaws armed with strong, sharp teeth and drowned in the water. Some prey may be wedged beneath submerged logs or rocks to be eaten a few days later. The Nile crocodile eats a large amount of carrion, and a dead hippopotamus may disappear within a few hours in a crocodile-infested river.

Crocodiles can't chew, instead they simply grip a piece of flesh in their jaws and spin around and round in the water until the chosen piece is torn off from the carcase.

The gharial of India, Nepal, Pakistan and Bangladesh has an extraordinarily-long snout armed with dozens of needle-sharp teeth. It feeds almost exclusively on fish that it first injures by lashing about sideways, open-jawed, in the rivers where it lives.

All crocodilians lay eggs, which they usually cover by a mound of earth or vegetation. Some species have been successfully bred and raised in captivity either on crocodile farms, where they are raised for their skin, or as captive-breeding projects for release into the wild. The majority of the twenty-two types are regarded as being endangered species.

The saltwater crocodile (above) is the world's largest crocodile. The American crocodile (below) is often confused with the alligator.

6
Tortoises, Turtles and Terrapins

Generally speaking, tortoises live exclusively on land, terrapins are found in and around fresh water and turtles are confined to the sea. Americans tend to call them all "turtles," while scientists group them all together as chelonians. They range in size from the musk terrapins (four inches) to the enormous leathery turtle (seventy inches in length) which, although it can weigh almost 1500 pounds, feeds almost exclusively on jellyfish.

The most striking feature of the chelonians is the hard shell that protects their body. This may be poorly developed, as in the softshell terrapins or the leathery turtle (hence the name), or else well developed, as in most land tortoises. Chelonians' limbs are well adapted to their particular function: turtles spend their lives swimming and are equipped with broad, flattened paddles, terrapins are usually carnivorous and have strong claws for tearing flesh, and tortoises have limbs that are shaped rather like those of an elephant: strong, thick and pillar-like for lifting the heavy shell well off the ground.

The chelonian shell is made of bone and covered in large, flat scales, or scutes. As the animal grows and stops growing depending on the seasons, ridges are laid down around the scutes, but these do not correspond to years and so they cannot be used to age the reptile.

All chelonians lay eggs, a single egg in the case of the curious, flattened pancake tortoise, and over a hundred in many of the marine species. The eggs have hard shells, like those of birds, and are laid in holes in soil or sand, destined to hatch two to five months later.

Many marine turtles return to the same beaches each breeding season to deposit their eggs, and probably the very beaches where the turtle itself hatched years earlier. Some may travel huge distances. Green turtles swim from their feeding grounds around the coast of Brazil to lay their eggs on the small, sandy beaches of Ascension Island. The island is barely ten miles across and yet they find their way to it over 1200 miles of ocean. They swim against the current and probably find their way following the "smell" of the volcanic island. The round trip takes many months and during this time the turtles do not feed, as they usually eat algae and eelgrass, foods which only grow in shallow waters close to the mainland.

Above left: giant tortoises mating in the Galápagos Islands. The box turtle (below) is a popular pet in America. The green turtle (facing page top) may migrate thousands of miles to its nesting beaches. Like all baby reptiles, red-bellied turtles (facing page bottom) are completely independent from the moment they hatch.

7

Venomous Reptiles

Two species of lizard and many species of snake possess a *venomous* bite. The lizards, the gila monster and beaded lizard, live in the deserts of the United States and Mexico and feed on birds' eggs, chicks, mammals and smaller reptiles. The venom sacs lie along the lizards' lower jaws and the venom is pumped along grooved teeth into the prey as the reptile bites. The bite causes death in small animals and intense pain in humans. The lizards are, however, brightly marked, having black and yellow or pink coloration as a warning that they should not be *molested.*

It has been estimated that 30-40,000 people die each year of snakebite, but many more are bitten and recover.

Venomous snake fangs are usually hollow and inject venom like a hypodermic syringe. The venom sacs, unlike those of the gila monster, are in the snake's upper jaw. Rattlesnakes and vipers have long fangs that are folded back when not in use, so only when the snake opens its mouth do the two teeth swing forward, ready for the strike. Cobras have small, needle-sharp fangs that are permanently erect, while some snakes, such as the boomslang, have their fangs at the back of

Below: a brightly colored coral snake in the rainforest of Costa Rica, and (bottom) a more soberly marked western rattlesnake.

the mouth and the venom is only injected into the prey when it is held firmly.

Some snake venoms act on the prey's nervous system, causing paralysis and death. Other venom acts on the victim's blood and circulatory system, destroying muscles and blood vessels. There are some species of snake whose venom is a mixture of the two types. As well as killing the prey, the venom continues to act within the animal's body even after it has been swallowed by the snake, breaking down tissues and assisting the snake's digestive system.

Snakes evolved venom and fangs in order to kill prey quickly. Many also use their bite to deter predators and some, such as the rattlesnake, warn enemies by rattling their special tail. Coral snakes rely on their bold black, yellow and red banding to warn other animals of their deadly, poisonous bite, and some harmless snakes have cashed in on this by having exactly the same markings, thereby appearing to be a venomous species.

The non-poisonous northern ringneck snake can pass as venomous by revealing its colorful belly scales to predators.

One species, the spitting cobra, uses its venom mainly for defense. Its hollow fangs have an opening halfway down them at the front, enabling the snake to eject a long stream of venom forward from each tooth. Its aim is perfect and it can easily hit an enemy right in the eyes, causing intense pain and even blindness.

8
Detecting Food

A snail-eater snake in the rainforest of Costa Rica

The vast majority of reptiles rely on sight, smell or sound, or a combination of all three, in detecting their prey. Chelonians use mainly their sight and sense of smell to detect food, whether it is animal or vegetable. Crocodilians use their eyes to detect live prey and their acute sense of smell to track down dead prey, which is often to be found a considerable distance from the rivers where they live. The primitive tuatara uses its eyes to discover moving prey, and it will try and eat almost any small, moving object. It is among the lizards and snakes, however, that we find the true masters of detecting prey. These reptiles usually have long, forked tongues that are regularly flicked in and out of the mouth when the animal is active. The tongue picks up tiny particles in the air or on the ground which are then transferred to the sensitive Jacobson's organs in the roof of the mouth. The minutest trace of the creature's prey can be detected in this way.

Some snakes and lizards have eyes that face forward, giving their owners binocular vision and enabling them to judge distances very accurately. Chameleons have remarkable eyes on the end of turrets. These turrets can move independently of each other, so while one eye is facing forward, looking at the prey, the other can be looking in all directions for danger. When the lizard is about to strike with its long, sticky tongue, both eyes are brought forward.

Some types of snake have a unique system of prey detection. Pit vipers and many species of pythons and boas possess special pits on either side of the head. In the pit vipers, these look like an extra pair of large nostrils, while in the boas and pythons there is a whole row along the lips. These pits are the most sensitive heat detectors known in nature. Each contains bundles of nerves that can detect minute differences in temperature – as little as a thousandth of a degree Celsius.

These snakes feed mainly on warm-blooded prey, such as mammals and birds, and are able to detect an animal by the heat given off by its body, even in complete darkness. As well as detecting prey, there are some reptiles that can actually attract prey. Some species of snake have brightly colored tips to their tails that they wriggle and wave about as if it were an insect. This attracts small lizards searching for food. As they approach, the snake pounces.

The North American alligator snapper terrapin looks like a huge, algae-covered rock as it sits on the bottom of the lake with its mouth wide open. On the base of its mouth there is a tiny, pink, worm-shaped lure that it wriggles to attract fish. As the fish nears the bait the terrapin snaps its jaws shut.

Above: a web-footed gecko eating a dune cricket in the Namib Desert, Namibia, South West Africa, and (below) a cat-eyed snake swallowing the eggs of a red-eyed leaf frog.

9

Defense

No other group of vertebrates exhibits such a wide range of *defense mechanisms* as the reptiles. The larger lizards and crocodilians lash out violently with strong jaws, claws and tail, while the chelonians simply retreat into their protective shell. One group, the box terrapins, have hinged flaps to their lower shell which they can close, completely sealing them inside.

Most snakes, whether venomous or not, will bite if molested, and many non-venomous species try to fool predators into thinking they are venomous either by their coloration or their behavior. Some snakes rely on *camouflage* to avoid being seen. Vine snakes are incredibly long and thin and very hard to see when they are motionless in a bush. There's camouflage too among the lizards. The chameleon is well known

The frilled lizard (above) exaggerates its size by raising the ruff of skin around its neck. Right: a southern copperhead beautifully camouflaged among dead leaves.

for its remarkable ability to change color and blend in with its surroundings.

The so-called ball python of West Africa rolls up into a tight ball when danger threatens, while the hog-nosed snake actually rolls over, mouth open and tongue hanging out, pretending to be dead to avoid being eaten. The "flying snakes" of Indonesia leap from their treetop homes to escape hawks. They can flatten their bodies and so slow down their fall to the ground.

Many lizards have horny spines covering their body to deter predators from eating them. The armadillo lizard of South Africa grabs its own tail in its jaws to form a thorny circle. The mastigives of Africa and Asia have thick, spiky tails that they lash out with when attacked, and they also use these tails to form a good barrier to their burrows as it prevents predators from entering

The Australian frilled lizard has a huge frill of skin around its neck, which it erects in the face of danger, much like its close relative the bearded dragon, which uses its spiky throat in the same way. If its bluff fails, the frilled lizard can always make good its escape traveling at high speed on its hind legs. The basilisk of Central America can also run in this *bipedal* fashion, reaching such a speed that it can run across the surface of a river to escape danger. For this ability to "walk on water," in some countries it is known as the "Jesus Christ" lizard.

One of the most remarkable ways in which lizards defend themselves is by dropping their tails. If a predator grabs a lizard as it is running away, it is likely to catch it by the tail. The reptile can, by a system of cracks in the bones in its tail, with a quick twitch of its muscles, throw off its tail, which nevertheless continues to wriggle. In many cases the predator will stop to eat the tail, thereby allowing the lizard to escape. A new tail will eventually grow, but it is rarely as well formed as the old one, as the join where the old tail broke away is usually clearly visible.

The western blue-tongued lizard uses its brightly colored tongue to scare off predators.

10
Reproduction

A grass snake with its eggs.

The primitive tuatara, the crocodilians and all the chelonians lay eggs, as do many snakes and lizards. Some lizards and snakes, however, retain these eggs within the body and give birth to live, fully-formed young. Chelonians, crocodiles and some lizards lay eggs with a hard, chalky shell, rather like a bird's egg. Other reptiles lay eggs with a tough, leathery shell. Eggs are normally either buried in holes in the ground or else hidden under rocks.

Turtles come ashore to lay their hundred or so eggs high up on the beach, while crocodilians often build up mounds of vegetation as nesting sites. Some lizards lay their eggs in termite hills, where the warmth of the colony helps to incubate them. The grass snake lays its eggs in compost heaps or piles of rotting vegetation, because the rotting process gives off heat and so warms the eggs.

The time it takes to incubate a reptile egg generally depends on the temperature around it, but two or three months is a good average. There are, however, some unusual exceptions. The tuatara's eggs take fifteen months or more to hatch, and chameleons emerge after twelve months of incubation. Monitor lizards' eggs develop over five to seven months, as do some tortoise species. On the other hand some snake eggs hatch only ten days after being laid, but these have already gone through a long period of development inside the female.

Those reptiles that incubate their eggs within the body have done away with shells altogether,

Left: a male anole lizard displays its spectacular dewlap. Below: hatching eastern hog-nosed snakes tear open their tough, leathery eggshells.

and instead the embryo is surrounded by a clear membrane which breaks open either just before or just after being laid. Reptiles that give birth to live young are termed "ovoviviporous" and the size of their broods depends on the species. The giant Solomon Island skink gives birth to a single, very large offspring, while the North American garter snake may have up to sixty writhing youngsters.

It has recently been discovered that in certain chelonians, crocodilians and lizards the sex of the hatchling is determined by the incubation temperature of the egg. In some species high constant temperatures (90°F and above) produce all males, while lower temperatures produce females. In other species these trends are reversed.

Even more bizarre are the small number of lizards and snakes around the world that reproduce "parthenogenetically." This means the population consists entirely of females that lay eggs that hatch out into more females. The male of the species simply does not exist.

Nevertheless, no matter how they are born, young reptiles are all completely independent from birth and do not rely on their parents for food.

11
Parental Care

Reptiles are not generally regarded as good parents. Whether hatched from eggs or born alive, the hatchlings are all ready to make their own way in the world and find food for themselves. Indeed, in some species the adults will not hesitate to make a meal of their own offspring, given the chance. Yet there are a few species that go to great lengths to protect their eggs and, sometimes, their offspring as well.

Many species of python wrap themselves around their eggs for the many months it takes them to hatch, leaving them only occasionally to drink or to bask in the sun. The female king cobra builds a complex mound of dead leaves as a nest for her eggs, and she then remains coiled on top of the nest to guard them from predators. One species, the Indian python, can actually produce a small amount of body heat by twitching its muscles, which helps the eggs to develop – a unique piece of behavior in the reptile world.

Some lizards, such as the Californian alligator lizard, are known to remain with their eggs until they hatch and many protect them against small animals. Parental care among the chelonians, however, is unknown, though the Burmese tortoise is known to bury its clutch of eggs in a mound of leaf litter and remain with them for several days.

It is the crocodilians, among the largest and most aggressive of reptiles, that do in fact make the best parents. The female Nile crocodile, for instance, goes to great lengths to protect her eggs and offspring; she chooses her nest site very carefully, not too close to the river's edge to run the risk of it being flooded, and yet close enough so that she can watch it from the water, chasing off predators such as monitor lizards and wild pigs. She watches the nest for the three months or more that it takes for the eggs to hatch, and may even go without food for this period.

Once they have broken their shells, the young crocodiles begin to call with a high-pitched "oink" and the female begins to dig out the nest. She then gently picks up the hatchlings in her enormous jaws and transports them, six or seven at a time, to the safety of the river. This prevents storks and herons snapping up the young, which would be possible if they made their own way down to the water. The way the female gently handles her young in her mouth is remarkable, especially when you consider that the ratio of the weight of adult to hatchling is four thousand to one.

Once she has carefully carried them all out of the nursery area she may remain with them for a further three or four months, until they are big enough to defend themselves against all but the largest predators.

An eastern garter snake (left) will give birth to over fifty young. Above: a Bynoe's gecko with its young. Facing page: young alligators at rest on their mother, who will protect them for the first few weeks of their lives.

12

Myths and Legends

Many myths and legends about reptiles have arisen over the centuries. Some originate from exaggerations, others out of inaccurate observations of animals in the wild, some from fear, and yet others out of ignorance.

The chameleon is one of the most feared lizards in Africa and yet it is completely harmless. From Morocco to South Africa the chameleon is treated with great respect as a certain death is said to follow its bite.

In Trinidad, the tree-living polycrus lizard is known to villagers as "Twenty-four Hours." Some people say this is because if one jumps on you, it will stay for twenty-four hours; others claim that if you are bitten by one you will die within a day. Polycrus is in fact a shy and gentle lizard that makes a good pet.

Perhaps more false stories about snakes have been told than about any other reptiles. As a result of their appearance and the ability of many species to kill humans, snakes have been worshipped or hated throughout the world. Pythons are sacred animals to the native peoples of Africa and Australia, while the Aztecs considered the rattlesnake to be a god. The cobra was a symbol of power to the Ancient Egyptians (it was an Egyptian cobra that bit Cleopatra), and intertwined snakes are still used in medicine as a sign of healing.

Sometimes it is difficult to see how the myths came about. The North American milk snake is said to get its name from its habit of suckling milk from cows at night. In medieval times it was believed that snakes would even attack small babies to obtain the milk they had just drunk. Some snakes were said to hypnotize their prey into immobility before striking – a result, no doubt, of the snake possessing an unblinking eye. There were even stories that venomous snakes exuded venom through their skin and that a person could die just by breathing within this fatal atmosphere!

The cobra (facing page) is one of the best known of the venomous snakes. The polycrus lizard (above) is also known as the twenty-four-hour lizard because anyone bitten by one is said to die within a day.

Even today, it is still widely believed that the female European adder will, if danger threatens, actually swallow all her young and then release them through her mouth when it is safe.

It is easy to see how such a story was invented. The adder gives birth to live, fully-formed young. Man's first reaction to this snake is usually to kill it on sight. A female, full of live young, might be mistaken for having swallowed them, rather than be thought to be just about to give birth. Exactly the same story is told about the North American rattlesnake, and it too gives birth to live young.

13
Reptiles and Man

In many parts of the world man's first reaction on seeing a snake is to kill it, whether it is venomous or not. In fact, in some southern states of America "Rattlesnake Round-ups" are still held every year. These events were originally organized to rid areas around schools and other public places of these potentially *lethal* reptiles, but today the event is big business and in many areas the snakes have become so scarce that they have to be imported from neighboring states to be slaughtered.

Once the thousands of rattlers have been rounded up they are killed, used in "skinning contests" and their flesh is eaten at barbecues. This is a senseless waste, and in many rattlesnake-free areas pests such as rats and mice (the prey of the rattler) are becoming a real problem.

In the same areas, venomous snakes such as rattlers, cottonmouths and copperheads are used in religious ceremonies, which involve the snakes being draped around a worshipper's head and neck. In one small village in the mountains of central Italy there is a snake-blessing ceremony in the church each year. The snakes, some venomous, are gathered from the fields and hillsides to be blessed. At one time they were released back into the wild, but now many are bought by snake dealers for the pet trade.

Green turtles are hunted for food by the Zamboanga boat people of the Philippines.

A commercial Nile crocodile farm at Lake Kariba, Zimbabwe.

Occasionally man falls prey to the larger crocodiles and snakes, but there are a large number of reptiles that are eaten by humans. Iguana is a favorite dish in Central America,and pythons are eaten in New Guinea. Spiny-tailed lizards are consumed in Morocco and other areas of North Africa and Aborigines still relish the Australian goanna (a monitor lizard).

Turtles and their eggs are eaten throughout the world, a fact that has led to their decline in recent years. Turtle farms have now been set up in many places, not only to release turtles back into the wild, but also to provide a source of turtle meat without damaging the wild population.

The same thing is happening with crocodiles, too, although not for their meat, but to meet the demand for their skins for the leather trade. Although these farms are in fact *exploiting* the reptiles, they may prove to be vital to their survival by releasing large numbers back into the wild – providing, of course, that their habitat has not been destroyed in the meantime.

Glossary

AMPHIBIAN - an animal that can breathe under water as well as in the air.

BIPEDAL - traveling on two legs.

CAMOUFLAGE - colored fur or skin that helps an animal remain hidden in its habitat.

CARNIVOROUS - living on meat.

DEFENSE MECHANISM - an immediate response to danger to avoid harm.

EVAPORATION - the changing of a liquid, often water, into vapor by warming.

EXPLOITATION - making use of something, such as land or animals, for selfish purposes.

HABITAT - the natural home of any plant or animal.

HERBIVOROUS - living by eating plants.

INSECTIVOROUS - living by eating insects

KERATIN - hard fiber of which nails, hooves, and claws are made.

LETHAL - capable of killing.

MOLEST - attack.

VENOMOUS - poisonous.

Picture Credits

Kathie Atkinson 11 *top*; Anthony Bannister 19 top; Stanley Breedon 2, 3, 5 *top*, 22; Mike Brown 15 *top*; Judd Cooney 16 *bottom*; Phil Devries 29; Michael Fogden 4 *top*, 5 *bottom*, 9, 10 *bottom right*, 11 *bottom*, 16 *top*, 18, 19 *bottom*, 24; Mark Hamblin 23; Breck P. Kent/Animals Animals 14 *bottom*; Michael Leach 31; Zigmund Leszczynski/Animals Animals 1, 6, 7, 10 *bottom left*, 15 *bottom*, 17, 21, 25 *right*, 26 *left*; Stan Osolinski 8, 12 *bottom*, 13 *bottom*; James Robinson 27; Maurice Tibbles 14 *top*, 30; Babs & Bert Wells 4 *bottom*, 26 *right*; Belinda Wright 12 *top*, 13 *top*, 20 *left*, 28.